HOW MP3 PLAYERS WORK

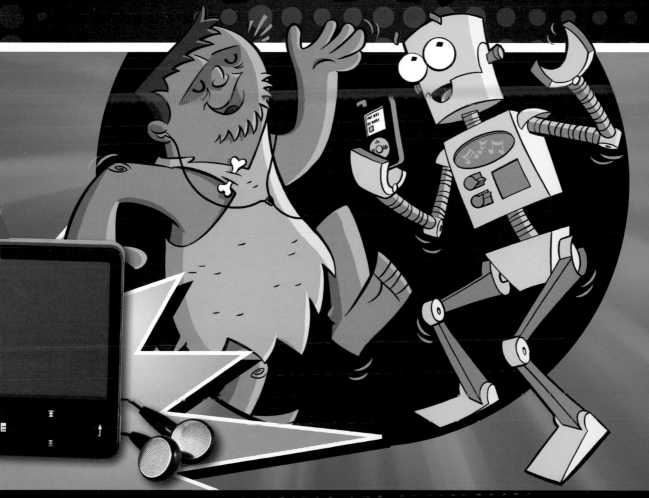

BY RYAN JACOBSON • ILLUSTRATED BY GLEN MULLALY

The Child's World®

Published by The Child's World®
1980 Lookout Drive • Mankato, MN 56003-1705
800-599-READ • www.childsworld.com

ACKNOWLEDGMENTS
The Child's World®: Mary Berendes, Publishing Director
Content Consultant: Paul Ohmann, PhD, Associate Professor
    of Physics, University of St. Thomas
The Design Lab: Design and production
Red Line Editorial: Editorial direction

LIBRARY OF CONGRESS
CATALOGING-IN-PUBLICATION DATA
Jacobson, Ryan.
  How MP3 players work / by Ryan Jacobson ;
illustrated by Glen Mullaly.
      p. cm.
  Includes bibliographical references and index.
  ISBN 978-1-60973-220-2 (library reinforced : alk. paper)
  1. MP3 players—Juvenile literature. 2. Sound—Recording
and reproducing—Juvenile literature. I. Mullaly, Glen, 1968–,
ill. II. Title.
  ML74.4.M6J33 2011
  006.5—dc22   2011013784

Photo Credits © iStockphoto, cover, 1, 9, 23 (right);
Shutterstock, 6 (right); Amanda Lewis/iStockphoto, 6 (left);
iStockphoto, 7 (bottom left), 14; Clark Music Co./Library
of Congress, 7 (top); Sven Hoppe/iStockphoto, 7 (bottom
right); Bart Broek/iStockphoto, 8 (left); Mike McCune/
iStockphoto, 8 (middle); Peter Gudella/Shutterstock, 8
(right); Jess Wiberg/iStockphoto, 10; Youssouf Cader/
iStockphoto, 13; Andres Balcazar/iStockphoto, 20; Brandon
Parry/iStockphoto, 22; Tomasz Darul/Shutterstock, 23 (left);
Jamie Duplass/iStockphoto, 28

Printed in the United States of America in Mankato,
Minnesota.
July 2011
PA02092

ABOUT THE AUTHOR
Ryan Jacobson is a successful author
and presenter. He has written nearly 20
children's books—including picture books,
graphic novels, chapter books and choose-
your-path books—with several more
projects in the works. He has presented
at dozens of schools, organizations,
and special events. Ryan lives in Mora,
Minnesota, with his wife Lora, sons Jonah
and Lucas, and dog Boo. For more about
the author, please visit his website at
www.RyanJacobsonOnline.com.

ABOUT THE ILLUSTRATOR
Glen Mullaly draws neato pictures for kids
of all ages from his swanky studio on the
west coast of Canada. He lives with his
awesomely understanding wife and their
spectacularly indifferent cat. Glen loves
old books, magazines, and cartoons, and
someday wants to illustrate a book on How
Monsters Work!

TABLE OF CONTENTS

CHAPTER ONE

PLAY THAT FUNKY MUSIC!

It's that time of year again. Your family is off to see your great-aunt Myrtle. The only stuff to do at her house is eat stewed onions and sit up straight. Worst of all, it takes a boring, five-hour drive to get there.

Bad news: Staying home is not an option. Good news: At least you have your music. But what do you feel like bringing? Oldies, country, rap, hip-hop, or maybe songs from a yodeling donkey? How will you ever decide?

Thanks to the wonders of MP3 players, you don't have to. You can bring them all—and more! (But if you plan on listening to that yodeling donkey, please keep the volume down.)

MP3 players put a world of music at your fingertips. You can store hundreds—even thousands—of songs in a machine that's smaller than a slice of pizza. One thing's for sure. This is not how your parents and grandparents listened to music. Let's take a quick look through the years to see how they rocked out.

People bought music mostly on records and cassette tapes. They usually listened to their favorite songs through large stereos that needed to be plugged in. Then the Sony Walkman came out in 1979. That let them hear their own cassettes on the go.

TIME LINE

325
Christianity officially becomes the religion of the Roman Empire. This leads to the spread of organized music throughout Europe.

850
Songs begin to feature melodies with harmonies, rather than single musical lines without backup.

ABOUT 1430
Folk music becomes popular.

1877
Thomas Edison invents the world's first record player.

The record player was new. Radio was new. In fact, the idea of hearing music through any sort of machine was new. For many people, music was something you made yourself. Or, you heard it live, either at church, at a special event, or from a family member.

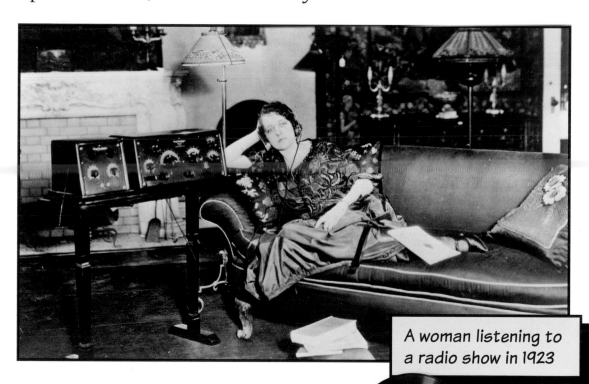

A woman listening to a radio show in 1923

1896
Radio is invented.

1920
The city of Pittsburgh, Pennsylvania, hosts the first commercial radio station.

1948
Columbia Records releases the "long-playing" record. It offers 44 minutes of music, far more than the previous standard of eight minutes.

1957
Sony invents the pocket transistor radio. For the first time ever, people can listen to music and information on the go.

1,000 YEARS AGO

A person might know a bit of folk music. But most songs were written and performed in honor of religious beliefs.

BACK TO TODAY

Since 1992, CDs have been king when it comes to buying music. But that trend is changing. Experts predict that MP3 sales will soon surpass CD sales. In fact, by the time you read this, they already might have!

1963
Philips Company introduces compact cassette tapes.

1979
Sony introduces the Walkman, a portable stereo.

1982
Compact discs (CDs) and CD players are first sold.

1989
A research company in Germany patents the MP3 format.

1992
More people buy CDs than cassette tapes for listening to music.

WE LOVE 'EM!

It's clear that MP3 players are the current trend. But why do we love them? Here are a few reasons:

- We can create our own song lists using our favorite songs.
- They fit in our pockets.
- They store tons of music.
- Many do more than just play songs. They show pictures and videos, work as cell phones, and connect to the Internet.

. . . and it plays music too!

But does it make fire?

1998
The world's first MP3 players are introduced.

1999
Napster begins its two-year reign as a source for free music downloads.

2001
Apple introduces its first iPod.

2003
The iTunes music store opens.

TODAY
Digital music and MP3s have taken the world by storm.

THANK YOU, MUSIC FANS

A shift in technology usually comes from large companies. For instance, listeners loved records until the music industry gave them cassette tapes. And they loved cassette tapes until the industry gave them CDs. But what's so amazing about the switch from CDs to MP3s? This movement was started by music fans! Thanks to computers and the Internet, song lovers fell for MP3s before the music industry was ready. This opened the door for online sites such as Napster, which started in 1999.

The idea behind Napster was that people could save their favorite songs from a CD onto a computer. Those songs could then be shared between computers. People could visit Napster, search for a song they wanted, and download it from someone else's computer. And it was all for free.

This process for sharing music was ruled illegal in 2001, and Napster was forced to shut down. But the technology shift was here to stay. Music fans wanted MP3s, and they wanted them by song, not by album. Today, we have sites such as iTunes and the new Napster, where MP3s can be bought legally.

CHAPTER TWO

EASY AS 1, 2, MP3

Music is a part of our everyday lives. We hear it in the car, on TV, and when we turn on our computers. Music can even affect how we feel. If you don't believe it, try watching a scary movie with the sound off. It's not so scary anymore, is it?

Nowadays, when we're talking about music, we're talking about MP3s. But do you really know what they are? Have you ever wondered how they work?

What's wrong? Do you miss your mommy?

No, it's this song!

The simplest way to understand an MP3 is to think of it as a computer file. If you use computers a lot, you probably know that a JPEG is a picture file and a DOC is a text file. In that case, an MP3 is—you guessed it—a sound file.

Now that you get what an MP3 is, let's step back and look at CDs. It'll help in understanding how an MP3 file works.

What's on That Disc?

Think of a CD like a suitcase. You pack it full of stuff. The stuff that gets put onto a CD is in code—it's **digital** information. This code is made of many, many 1s and 0s. The numbers form patterns, like 11100011 or 10100111. The computer understands those patterns. Believe it or not, to a CD player or a computer, a song is just a bunch of 1s and 0s.

We can't put too much stuff onto a CD. It will get full. The file size of a typical song on a CD is about 60 megabytes (MB), and a CD can hold around 15 songs.

Wait a minute? 60 MB? When it comes to computers and the Internet, that's huge! It could take forever to download a song that big! Plus, an MP3 player couldn't store thousands of 60-MB songs. There's not enough room. But MP3s have a secret to their success. . . .

1s and 0s form endless patterns of digital data on a CD.

PLAY THAT CD

When a song gets recorded, it becomes digital **data** stored on a computer. How does that data get onto a CD? A tiny laser beam cuts it onto the bottom of the disc. You probably can't tell by looking, but the bottoms of CDs are actually covered with bumps and grooves.

What happens after the disc goes into a player? The player spins the disc very fast, while a low-powered laser shoots it. A laser is a special kind of light beam. This laser hits the bumps and grooves, and it reflects back into the player. This reflected laser communicates digital information to the player. The player then changes that digital information into electricity. The electricity is sent to speakers or headphones, which turn it into music.

A laser beam cuts data onto a CD.

CHAPTER THREE

HOW DOES IT WORK?

MP3s

All right, so what's that secret about MP3s? It boils down to one word: **compression**. But what does that mean? Well, in this case, it means making those 60-MB music files much, much smaller.

For a minute, think of a music file as a book. The thickness of the book depends on the number of pages. And the number of pages depends on how many words and pictures are in the story. If we take out a bunch of words and pictures, we can make the book smaller—or compress it.

What are you doing?

Compression!

Music files work in a similar way. Instead of pages, a music file is made up of frames. And instead of words and pictures, each frame is filled with music data. So how do we compress a music file? By taking out some of the music data!

We can get that 60-MB file down to 4 or 5 MB. That's right—90 percent of the file is taken away. But, believe it or not, the compressed song still sounds an awful lot like the original. Plus, those small files are easier to download off the Internet. It means your MP3 player can store tons of music!

What are you?

A GIG'S WORTH

In an MP3 player, 64 MB of space is about one hour of music. One gigabyte (GB) of space equals 1,024 MB. And, 1,024 divided by 64 equals 16. That means an MP3 player can hold about 16 hours of music for every 1 GB of space it has.

1 GB = 16 HOURS

FOR BETTER OR FOR WORSE

So far, MP3s sound perfect. They're better than CDs in every possible way, right? Not so fast. There is a downside to MP3s. Once again, it comes down to that magical word, compression.

Let's say you have a message to give your friend. You want to tell him, "I am coming over to your house today. I hope that is okay with you. Please let me know." It's a simple message, just 19 words. But let's say you're not going to call or e-mail him. You're going to text him.

Texts are usually much shorter than 19 words, so

What are you doing?

Oh, I'm just remembering the good old days.

you need to change your message. It might become something like, "Coming over, k?"

Look at that: You just compressed your message from 19 words to three! Both messages mean the same thing, but 16 words are gone forever. No one will ever know what they were.

Is that a big deal? Probably not. But the same rule applies to MP3s. When music gets compressed into an MP3, some of the data is taken away—and lost forever. That doesn't mean words get removed or the song becomes shorter. Instead, the music loses some of its sound quality. The song remains the same, but it doesn't sound quite as good anymore.

Okay, we've learned that MP3s are a type of computer file. That must mean an MP3 player is a computer, right? Let's take a quick peek at how computers and MP3 players compare:

- A computer must have a way for you to put data inside it. Does an MP3 player let you put data inside? Of course! If you couldn't add songs to your MP3 player, it wouldn't be much use.

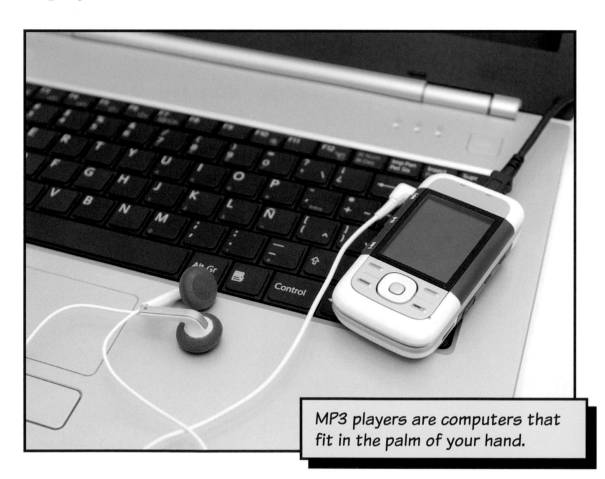

MP3 players are computers that fit in the palm of your hand.

An MP3 player has a microprocessor, just like a computer.

- A computer has **memory**, which allows you to store data inside it. How about an MP3 player? Yes! Why would you put songs into the MP3 player if it didn't remember them?

- A computer is a machine that processes information. Does an MP3 player process information? You bet it does! The player reads the digital information inside MP3 files and turns it into music.

- A computer needs to get the data out again so you can use it. What about an MP3 player? Yep—it outputs data in the form of sound.

TYPES OF MP3 PLAYERS

There are two basic kinds of MP3 players. The biggest difference between them is how many songs they hold. Well, that and how much they cost.

1. Flash memory player: This is the smallest and lightest kind of player, which makes it good for working out. Some of the best flash players hold up to 2,000 songs.

2. Hard drive player: This one is a little bigger and heavier. Some of these players can hold up to 40,000 songs. People who want to use their MP3 players for everything from music to pictures to videos prefer hard drive players.

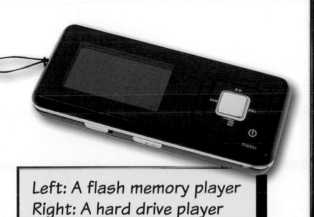

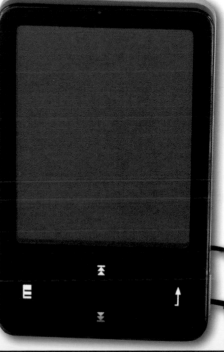

Left: A flash memory player
Right: A hard drive player

CHAPTER FOUR

TAKE IT APART

1. The data port allows the MP3 player to be connected to a computer, usually with a USB cable. MP3s are sent into the player through this port.

2. Once inside, MP3s are stored in the player's memory.

3. The playback controls allow users to tell the MP3 player what to do: play, fast forward, skip to the next song, and more.

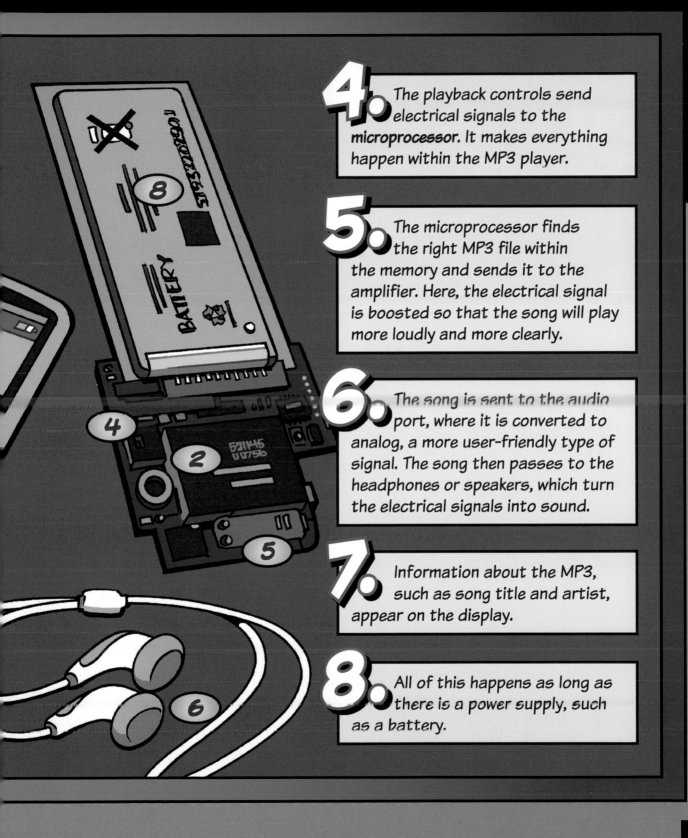

4. The playback controls send electrical signals to the **microprocessor**. It makes everything happen within the MP3 player.

5. The microprocessor finds the right MP3 file within the memory and sends it to the amplifier. Here, the electrical signal is boosted so that the song will play more loudly and more clearly.

6. The song is sent to the audio port, where it is converted to analog, a more user-friendly type of signal. The song then passes to the headphones or speakers, which turn the electrical signals into sound.

7. Information about the MP3, such as song title and artist, appear on the display.

8. All of this happens as long as there is a power supply, such as a battery.

CHAPTER FIVE

FILL 'ER UP!

So you have an MP3 player, and you want to get music on there. Well, this is where the fun begins. You get to make your own song lists!

Most people start by digging through the music they own. After all, you can convert CD tracks to MP3s and save them onto your computer. This process is called **ripping**. Once an MP3 is on your computer, it's easy to move it onto an MP3 player.

Many music fans will also visit an online music store, such as iTunes. Here, users can find their favorite songs and buy them for around $1 each. Once purchased, the song files download to the computer. From there, you can move them onto an MP3 player.

Some music stores—such as the new Napster—offer subscriptions. For a flat monthly fee (usually under $10), you can download as many songs as you want. But most of the songs will only work as long as you keep paying the monthly fee. Once you quit, the songs won't work anymore.

Some MP3 players let you download music wherever you are.

Of course, some MP3 players allow you to skip the computer altogether. These players record songs directly from CD players. Or, they connect to the Internet—and online music stores—themselves.

HEY, THAT'S NOT FREE!

Imagine that you wrote a cool song, and you worked out a deal with a record company to produce the song and help you sell it. You wrote the song, right? So, in a way, you own it. Whenever your song is sold, you're supposed to get a piece of the profit. Now, imagine that your song becomes a huge hit. Kids everywhere are copying it and passing it along to their friends. Some kids are still paying to get your song—but many aren't.

That would probably make you mad, right? A lot of people would agree with you. They think music needs to be protected. That's why most of the songs people download come with special software to do just that. This software keeps track of things like how many times the song gets moved onto an MP3 player. If the song gets copied too many times, it won't allow itself to be copied anymore.

CHAPTER SIX

TWINKLE, TWINKLE LITTLE STAR

Thanks to MP3 players, all of your favorite songs fit inside your pocket—but there's even more great news that you might not have thought about. Because of MP3s, anyone who wants to become a recording artist can!

Tell the truth. You've dreamed of being a rock star. You've even thought about making your own album. Well, guess what? It's as easy as this:

1. Record your own songs, which you can do through a computer.
2. Convert your songs into MP3s.
3. Pass along your MP3s to all of your friends.

Many musicians also sell their own songs on sites like iTunes.

That's not how it was done 15 years ago. If singers wanted to make their own albums, it would cost them thousands of dollars. Now, thanks to MP3s, it costs almost nothing!

WORDS TO KNOW

compression (kuhm-PRESH-un): Compression reduces the size of a computer file by removing some of its information. MP3 files are created by compression.

data (DAY-tuh or DAH-tuh): Data is another word for information. Computers and MP3 players process and store huge amounts of data.

digital (DIHJ-uh-tuhl): *Digital* refers to a way of coding information so that computers can read it. MP3 files contain digital information that gets converted into music by a player.

memory (MEM-uhr-ee): Memory is an MP3 player's storage space. The more memory a player has, the more songs it can hold.

microprocessor (my-kroh-PROS-uhs-uhr): The microprocessor is the "brains" of an MP3 player. It makes everything happen in order for a song to play.

ripping (RIHP-ing): Ripping is the process where CD tracks are converted to MP3 files and saved onto a computer. Ripping is just one way to put music onto an MP3 player.

Visit our Web site for links about how MP3 players work: childsworld.com/links

Note to Parents, Teachers, and Librarians: We routinely verify our Web links to make sure they are safe and active sites. So encourage your readers to check them out!